Too Jagged to Hold

Kristen Hornung

For everyone who has asked themselves,
Am I recovered yet?

CONTENTS

Author's Note on Content and Context

Warning: This collection contains themes of sexual violence, self-harm, emotional abuse, and grief.

When I was seventeen years old, I was raped. At the time, I didn't know how to cope, how to grieve, or how to heal. The sense of loss and isolation I felt was hard to articulate. I didn't yet understand what long-term recovery might look like for me. Talking openly about what I had experienced was incredibly difficult, and sometimes it still is. Fortunately, I've always loved reading and writing. Poetry became a way to explore and express my inner world without holding back.

I wrote the first draft of "Seventeen" after I reported the rape at the police station and was waiting at a table. I didn't have any other paper in my purse at the time, but I needed to write, so I unfolded gum wrappers one at a time and wrote on them instead. Even though I revised this poem prior to including it in this collection, I didn't alter the original style and structure. I wanted to allow it to stand out from the rest as a product of my seventeen year old mind.

The effects of trauma didn't appear all at once. Over time, I came to recognize its impact across nearly every part of my life: my relationships with others, my relationship with my body, my identity, and my mental health. I'm deeply grateful for the therapists, health-care providers, teachers, friends, family, and recovery communities who have supported me along the way.

Today I find meaning, purpose, and joy in the life I've built. I'm nearly forty years old, married with two children, and work in a career I care deeply about. And still, the wound remains. It no longer defines me, but I've learned I need to tend to it with care.

This collection is rooted in my experience of trauma and recovery. While many of the poems explore themes of resilience, healing, embodiment, and renewal, they also include autobiographical and metaphorical depictions of trauma, dissociation, and emotional pain that may be activating or distressing for some readers. Please take care as you move through these pages.

The Alchemist's Journey
Part I: Putrefaction

We begin where nobody wants to; lost,
alone in the dark underground,
with all that's been discarded,
suffocating in the stench of
sour sweat, rotting leaves,
overflowing toilets

you have been stuck knee-deep in loam
for long enough to question the
boundaries of your flesh,
what is within, what is without,
who you are if your successes
and failures do not matter

a blue orb—a flame's heart? a moon?
flickers on the horizon, reminding you of
sweet milk breath, a hand in your hair

you shake your legs free and begin to walk
directionless, just anywhere but here

THE TENSION

Slide until the hook bites,
drags you through the cold blue

trace the line back,
feeling for your edges

orient to what separates
sun, water, air, flesh

question if you are the fisherman
or the fish

THE MARK

Your lover arrives at the
café empty-handed,
offering you nothing;
no sweet to savor later,
no trinket to treasure,
not even a solitary
bud barbed with thorns

he weaves a story about
forgetting his wallet,
but his words tangle,
land like a lie—
you would wager
he remembered to tuck
a joint and a lighter
into his pockets

the pancakes piled
in front of you shine
with butter and
whipped cream,
yet they remain
cotton dry on the inside;
you cut smaller bites,
force them down

he twists a lock of
golden hair behind his ear,
widens his sky-blue eyes,
smiles like he's sharing
a secret only you
will understand

his beauty is louder
than the rain pelting
the window,
brighter than the
fluorescent lights glaring
down on your table,
and so persuasive
you imagine him
saying what you
need to hear
as he drains his
cup of coffee

INFLUENCED

The claws sink into you painlessly
like the most subtle of splinters,
drawn deep, then deeper

being unable to feel their grip
is no kindness; I've never met
someone who could
resist a ghost

how could you know which faces
are real, which beliefs have
grown poisonous in the garden
of your mind, or where their lies
begin and your truths end

SEVENTEEN

9:15 p.m.

these gum wrappers hold answers
(dare i hope?)
i'm slumped over the table, writing in
mad desperation, wondering what
steps carried me here

pen, i will follow you through
these dead fields

1.
i saw you
curly brown hair, dark eyes
good smile, soft voice

i am stuck at the library
comfortable amid novels
molding a first impression
bright with laughter

2.
what words did we speak?
a boyfriend girlfriend slush
of pretendings
and the *i love you*
that taught me there are
some things worse
than nothing

for instance:

3.
seeing myself
   my legs
red buds on the
   wood floor

crouching in pain and silence
   ashamed

4.
the cruel lesson of vulnerability
the tumbling of sins
an attacked body
a failed mind
the tragedy of
my human heart

5.
the unraveling of what i am

the desire for a wildflower afternoon
where creation and expansion
set me at the end of the periscope
until i saw the other boy and me
(not together, but there)

he is not to be had
and i am here, hailing tears
that won't come

i do not want this
part of me to die

i love you, i love you
forgive my desperation
blame my pen
for opening avoided fields

i did not want this death
to include you

BREAK

Thoughts surge like water
breaching a failed dam;
a bracing, no-end-in-sight torrent
threatening to drown her

on her knees, she presses her forehead
into the scratched wood floor,
hard, then harder, trying to feel

the real, the relief of a limit
to the violent flood,
the solace of being held,
even if only by the ground

MISSING YOU

I inhaled you today
a blizzard of icicles
plummeting to violet,
blistering my lungs,
unhinging my bones

do you remember our night
in the orchard?
citrus air, dust,
our shadows merging,
I lost myself in you
and starlight

I precipitate on a
glittering white wasteland
blue beads weigh down
my frosted eyelashes,
my body is frozen trees
and sleeping lakes

to thaw I invite
pain to bite me,
swallow what burns,
recruit others to
help me escape
the end of this story

SURRENDER

As Grandpa's body wanes in bed,
the hours bleeding together,
he releases his routines,
accepts the help he never wanted

his heart drifts in and out of rhythm,
the oxygen tank wheezes,
afternoon sunlight filters
through the trees he planted
thirty years before,
warming the room

when I take his hand
his grip anchors me,
and I see us as two orbs
bobbing in a dark sea,
tethered together by
a pearlescent shimmer

I ask if he's dying;
he answers, "Not yet."

later I'll walk through the yard
to say goodbye to his roses,
the wishing willow,
the creeping strawberries,

Grandma's sun-bleached
statues of cherubs,
broken wind chimes,
the patio tables now coated
in a thin layer of grime

for decades our family gathered
around the pool to celebrate holidays with
platters holding Fritos and guacamole,
Grandpa's barbecue baked beans,
black olives, sweet pickles, shrimp and
cocktail sauce with horseradish on
ice, and German chocolate cake

on a recent visit Grandma offered
my daughter a cold, slimy lump
of spaghetti from a Tupperware,
a room-temperature, half-eaten
jar of grape jelly, a bag of truffles,
a spoon she shined on her shirt

now Grandma mostly remains
in the chair kitty-corner
to his motorized bed,
cradles her black leather purse, and
asks me about the baby in my belly,
over and over

he grows concerned whenever
she leaves his sight;
if it was only a matter of fighting,
he would stay alive

THE CYCLE

Flames lap up every limb within reach
roots smolder, community disintegrates
    How do you define a body?
smoke climbs, ash settles

crystals bloom in darkness
atoms align, faces reflect
    What is meant to be?
diamonds cut, graphite slips

of skin, scale, feather, fur, or shell
cells hunger, blood exchanges
    How do you measure a life?
carbon returns

THRESHOLD

The last thing you do before you leave
home is tell yourself you can
come back for more

look back, see yourself as you were
a child so filled with dreams
you seemed likely to lift off
the ground, be carried away
by a ribbon of air unspooling
through an open window

look back, see your parents
as they were,
fickle gods fleshing out your map
of the world,
they turned the steering wheel
while you gazed
at all the wrong things;
streetlights blurred by rain

look back, clock the spent time,
in church you held salvation against
the roof of your mouth until it dissolved,
squeezed a quarter in your hand,
thought about the donut
you could buy later

look back, question
what has changed,
who has changed,
hug the bag of 80s plastic
serving trays and plates against your chest,
remind yourself this isn't home anymore,
what you need isn't here

the last thing you do before you leave
home is tell yourself you can
come back

THE ALCHEMIST'S JOURNEY

PART II: DISSOLUTION

White the shade of polished bone
blots out the night,
cleaves to you like snowfall,
numbing your skin

you fear erasure,
of becoming only as visible as
wind rattling a tree,
but you are dissolving

the cold is sharp as searing heat;
in another time you tended
a solution boiling in a crucible
until yolk-yellow crystals formed

now it is your turn;
the lines you drew to define
yourself wash away;
you change phase

USED

He drove his new car recklessly, testing
limits on the lonely desert road
until he spotted me,
long abandoned to the dust
yet still gleaming like gold,
and pulled over

dirt puffed up around his scuff-free
leather boots, his face reddened
from the heat, but he thought only
of the ways he could use me

he didn't realize I was nothing
but cheap scrap metal,
too broken to be worth fixing,
too jagged to hold,
and unwilling to be forced
into the back seat

my edges became teeth at his touch,
contracting around his hands,
climbing up his sweat-slick forearms
as he grunted, tried to pull away,
shook, shouted, screamed,
popped, cracked, leaked,
crumpled

his cries quieted as I
climbed behind the wheel

HEAVENLY BODIES

The planet and her moon
  mother and daughter
spinning
  the tension between
  holding on and letting go

tidally locked
shaping, pacing
  she says, I will love you
  forever

invisibly bound
  even when drawn apart
even when drifting farther away
  their resonance persists

they dance across the distance

INTO THE WATER

When she swims, her loose hair gathers
the yellow palm tree flowers,
but not the bees;
I scoop them out of her path
with my cupped hands

every time she surfaces for a breath,
she sputters through the strands,
refuses the scrunchie on my wrist

she asks me to stay close,
although I think we both know
she is strong enough now

to mermaid dive to the bottom,
starfish float in place,
to make it to the side if she tires
while swimming the whole length

almost six years old—
watching her, I remember
how she used to cling
and curl her tiny fists around
my swimsuit straps

when I tell her we need to dry off
she glides to the stairs in the
shallow end, I follow

instead of climbing out, she
pulls a lock of hair from her mouth,
smiles. "Can I have
a few more minutes
to play Ice Cream Shop?"

weary of negotiating everything,
yet relieved she still loves our old game,
I agree and crouch beside her,
angling my back to keep
her face in the shade

"Do you want the unicorn surprise?"
she taps a pearl-colored tile.
"It's every single flavor, with
pieces of cone, and whipped cream,
and sprinkles, with a cherry on top."

"Yes please, two scoops."

she splashes and twirls, then
flourishes her arm. "Here you go."

as I accept the pretend treat,
her fingertips kiss mine,
and I wish I could freeze
this sweet moment in time

In Memory Of

I found an obituary for the man
who raped me nineteen years ago,
when I was only seventeen,
and all I could think about was how
his mother might have reconciled his fate

how she must grieve the loss
of the boy she loved,
the man she imagined he
might become, and the man
he proved himself to be

I didn't feel anything right away,
not even the relief I always imagined,
but much later, I found myself disturbed,
like water churned up by a storm;
a cloudy, nonsense mess of debris,
memories bubbling up...

even after all these years of
trying to heal my body and mind,
I can only expel these words with
the curtains drawn tight,
the noise machine humming,
and my youngest nestled
against me, dreaming

Will it ever feel safe to speak about this?

on the hardest days
time slows, skips, stops;
my breathing falls out of rhythm,
fears amplify, become strange;
I misplace my headphones, my keys;
I stumble and bump into everything

until his phantom chokehold loosens,
then I once again find my way back
to where a soft, sweaty cheek rests
on my arm, gentle pulses of air from
the ceiling fan wash across my skin,
and these words stare back at me

THE SPIRAL

You climb flight after flight of stairs
even though you yearn to slow,
to linger, or turn back around—
you can't comprehend what
compels you to keep going,
the circularity of the
ticking clock, and
how the years
add up

you dream of entering one of the
countless unlit rooms,
of sorting through
what has been
abandoned

how good it would feel
to find something to
hold on to,
an anchor for
your empty hands

each landing is an echo
of places you called home,
reminding you of how you
have grown and the ways

time has shaped you

like the pair of dust-softened
blue jeans you once found
behind a stack of faded
spiral notebooks

the longer you stared
at the loose threads
across the knees,
the easier it became
to imagine yourself
at seventeen,

turning in front
of the mirror,
anticipating
your crush's eyes
on you later,
his hands grasping
your belt loops,
tugging—

you can feel it now
so vividly and yet
you are here,
climbing,
always climbing,
and you are alone

trapped in this
house-not-quite-a-home,
lost in the space

between your memories and
the truth, who you were
and who you are,
and who you've
longed to be

THE LONG WAY

Depart before dawn,
follow the dirt path
into the valley
hidden by fog

where rust-brown and
dusty-gray coyotes glide
through the chaparral,
where every breath burns
like a gulp of ice water

the river drowns out the
crunch of your footsteps

anise chokes the trail,
releasing the scent of
black licorice as you
shoulder past

until you reach the drop-off,
where you have no choice
but to pause:

your heart thumps in your ears,
condensation and sweat
drip from your chin,

and your muscles shiver

yet your soul yearns
to follow the river over
the edge

through the ravine bristling
with cottonwoods, willows,
bamboo

under roads, across
land dotted with
orange and lemon trees
and ranch-style mansions

to where it joins with the sea—
but you know your limits

instead, you wait until the sun crests
the ridge and cascades over you,
warming your cheeks and
the tip of your nose,
melting away the fog

then, despite the wanderlust
taking root in your soul,
you knock the clumps of mud
from your boots, turn around,
and venture home—
the long way

THE LIGHT WITHIN

The deep freeze rolls in with the
numbing fog, penetrates the
stone walls you've built to shield
your straw house, pursues
you to the blazing hearth

when you fall to your knees you
feel nothing, as if you are wearing
the body of a stranger, yet when
you reach out, your hands move
into the dancing light

you've too often neglected the
ever-hungry flame, but now you
see it is a beating heart, what
makes a house a home, and a
guide for the darkest of nights

THE THREAD

In the unraveling of all that I am,
I find what led me here:
the tumbling of sins,
an attacked body,
a fragmented mind,
the tragedy of my
human heart

truth is, I don't want
to begin again

if I could, I would suspend
the sun in the sky,
weave the clouds together
to make you a bed

I've been craving a glitch,
to swoon out of time,
to fall between your lips;
a fix for the numbing hours

What can I say? I need that kind
of love, the ecstasy of hovering
outside my mind, of being bare

Do you know how much
you mean to me?
when I was lost in death,
reduced to an echo of who I am,
I found your soul, and it
guided me home

CONIUNCTIO

Unmoored from my body, I floated in;
ocean-blue walls, frothy white carpet, and,
behind her, a window to her garden...
when I started to fade, she held my hand

hour after hour we met at the border
to conjure my dreams of twisted vases,
pet fish languishing in murky water,
snakes outgrowing, escaping their cages

we parleyed with monsters to broker peace,
shattered mirrors that masqueraded as soul,
unwound my story until it released,
giving me the chance to choose a new role

before she passed, I found gifts in my scars—
when I hold space for others, I sense she's not far

FOR YOU

I love you the way you love the ocean;
ever-loyal, returning day after day,
delighting in even the worst of waves

as much as you crave the rush
of saltwater, sun, and sand,
I hunger for quiet alcoves and the
safe companionship of words,
the way I can dive into a story,
lose myself among the pages

I've wondered if your true home
hides beyond the breakers—
in another life, I am brave enough
to swim out and meet you there

ENOUGH

Tell me what it is to live—
I only know how to dream,
spin stories, tie knots,
keep distance, climb ladders,
cook to eat, clean messes,
stare at the moon, walk alone
in the rain, listen with feeling,
peek at the sun, sit with
shadows, pull loose threads,
and ask too many questions

THE ALCHEMIST'S JOURNEY

PART III: THE SORCERER'S STONE

You crawl out of blood-warm water
onto a mound of ocher earth where
a solitary black tree stands tall,
bare arms raised, reaching out;
a lightning strike in reverse

you retreat from the orange eye
of the sun, sit with your back
resting against the blistered bark,
lick salt from your lips

seaweed bristles in your hair,
mud dries in the grooves of your skin,
mapping spent time

the scent of roses
pulls at you like a current;
you dig your fingers into
the soil, think of gold
as your vision inverts

you see yourself as you are—
King but also Queen, Babe,
Crone, Clown, Virgin, Sage…
not one truth, but many

you have heard rumors of
transcendence, but you have
dreamed of an infinite tower
bridging land and sky

of an egg as hard as stone,
of raking compost into a
garden bed, of bending
mirrors to fit your reflections

and all you know of endings
is how to begin again

Acknowledgments

Dear reader, thank you for taking the time to read my work. I deeply appreciate you. If you are in recovery or identify as a trauma survivor, I hope these words have resonated with you and helped parts of you feel seen.

If you would like to help others find my work, please consider sharing an honest review online, it can really make a difference.

I want to extend heartfelt thanks to my family, friends, previous teachers and mentors, and all those who have supported my healing journey and passion for writing.

I am especially grateful to my critique partner and fellow author, Robert Harrison, for all of his support and for helping me publish this book.

Thank you to my editor, Meghan Fandrich, for working with me to polish my manuscript.

Collaborating with Jessica Cvilo on cover design was an amazing experience.

The wonderful writers and helpful leader of an open writing group held by San Diego Writers, Ink, encouraged me to make time and space for my writing. I am very grateful for their support.

I appreciate the following publications for previously publishing my poems:

"Threshold" was published in the *San Diego Poetry Annual*, 2024-2025 edition, in March 2025.

"Into the Water" and "The Long Way" were published by *Kelp Journal* on September 21, 2023.

"In Memory Of" and "Coniunctio" were published by Beyond the Veil Press in the *Dear Survivor: reclaim the light: Anthology of Poetry & Art by Survivors of Sexual Assault* in 2024.

ABOUT THE AUTHOR

Kristen Hornung (she/hers or no pronouns) is a writer from Encinitas, California. Her poetry and prose have appeared in *Psychological Perspectives, Zooscape, Kelp Journal, Beyond the Veil Press, San Diego Poetry Annual*, and elsewhere.

Kristen earned a BA in chemistry from Brown University, an MA in counseling from the University of San Diego, and a PhD in depth psychology with an emphasis in depth psychotherapy from Pacifica Graduate Institute.

Kristen holds a deep belief in the power of storytelling for reclaiming one's voice, healing, and connection. She identifies as a person in recovery. *Too Jagged to Hold* is her debut poetry collection.

Connect with her by visiting her author website, where you can sign up for her newsletter to access free bonus poems at https://kghornung.com/